SEA LIFE

JELLYFISH

by **Mari Schuh**

Consulting Editor:
Gail Saunders-Smith, PhD

Consultant:
Jody Rake, Member,
Southwest Marine Educators Association

CAPSTONE PRESS
a capstone imprint

Pebble Plus is published by Capstone Press,
1710 Roe Crest Drive, North Mankato, Minnesota 56003
www.capstonepub.com

Library of Congress Cataloging-in-Publication Data
Schuh, Mari C.
Jellyfish / by Mari Schuh
p. cm.—(Pebble plus. Sea Life)
Summary: "Describes the characteristics, food, habitat, and behavior of jellyfish"—Provided by publisher.
Audience: 4-8
Audience: K to grade 3.
Includes bibliographical references and index.
ISBN 978-1-4914-6043-6 (library binding)
ISBN 978-1-4914-6063-4 (eBook PDF)
1. Jellyfishes—Juvenile literature. I. Title.
QL377.S4S38 2016   2014049350

Editorial Credits
Elizabeth R. Johnson, editor; Aruna Rangarajan, designer;
Kelly Garvin, media researcher; Tori Abraham, production specialist

Photo Credits
Corbis/Ingo Arndt, 19; iStockphoto/mauinow1, cover; SeaPics.com: Bob Cranston, 9, Masa Ushioda, 11; Shutterstock:
dibrova, 13, Ethan Daniels, 5, Godruma, cover (background), holbox, 12, Jorg Hackemann, 21, Lana Rattanko, 7, Richard A.
McMIllin, 15, Vlad61, 17

Design Elements: Shutterstock: Jiri Vaclavek, Khoroshunova, SusIO, Vectomart

Note to Parents and Teachers

The Sea Life set supports national science standards related to life science. This book describes and
illustrates jellyfish. The images support early readers in understanding the text. The repetition of
words and phrases helps early readers learn new words. This book also introduces early readers
to subject-specific vocabulary words, which are defined in the Glossary section. Early readers may
need assistance to read some words and to use the Table of Contents, Glossary, Read More, Internet
Sites, and Index sections of the book.

Printed in China by Nordica
0415/CA21500542
032015   008837NORDF15

Table of Contents

Life in the Ocean 4

Up Close 8

Finding Food 14

Life Cycle 18

Glossary 22

Read More 23

Internet Sites 23

Index 24

Life in the Ocean

Jellyfish are not what they seem.
Don't let their name fool you.
Jellyfish are not fish at all!

5

Jellyfish are ocean animals.
They float in oceans
around the world.

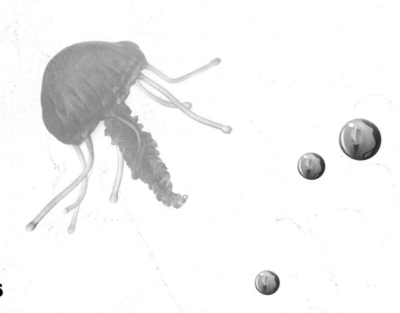

Up Close

Jellyfish are many sizes.

Some are as small as a pea.

Others are bigger than a person.

They can be 7 feet

(2 meters) wide.

Bright colors cover some jellyfish.
Other jellyfish are clear.
Some jellyfish even glow!

11

Jellyfish do not have bones.
They have soft bodies shaped
like bells or umbrellas.
They open and close their
bodies to move.

Finding Food

Jellyfish have many tentacles. The tentacles sting prey with poison. Once stung, the prey cannot swim away.

The tentacles pull the prey
into the jellyfish's mouth.
Jellyfish eat fish and plankton.

Life Cycle

Female jellyfish make eggs.

The eggs later grow into polyps.

Polyps live on the ocean floor.

Young jellyfish grow
from the polyps.
They break away and
move on their own.
In a few weeks, they
become adult jellyfish.

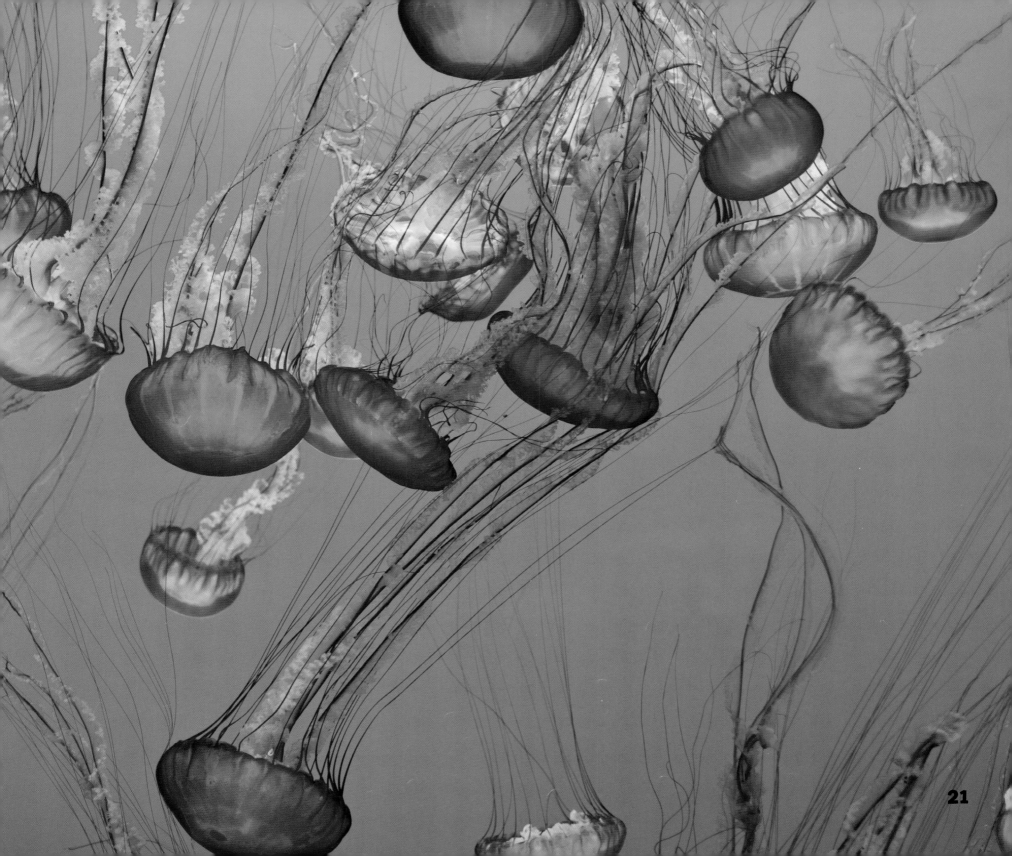

Glossary

plankton—animals and plants, usually tiny, that drift or float in oceans and lakes

poison—a substance that can kill or harm an animal or person

polyp—a jellyfish at the stage of development during which it lives on the ocean floor

prey—an animal hunted by another animal for food

tentacle—a long, flexible body part used for moving, feeling, and grabbing

Read More

Hughes, Catherine D. *First Big Book of the Ocean.*
National Geographic Little Kids. Washington, D.C.:
National Geographic Kids, 2013.

Meister, Cari. *Jellyfish.* Life Under the Sea. Minneapolis:
Bullfrog Books, 2015.

Raum, Elizabeth. *Box Jellyfish.* Poisonous Animals.
Mankato, Minn.: Amicus, 2016.

Internet Sites

FactHound offers a safe, fun way to find Internet sites
related to this book. All of the sites on FactHound have
been researched by our staff.

Here's all you do:

Visit *www.facthound.com*

Type in this code: 9781491460436

Index

bodies, 12

bones, 12

colors, 10

eggs, 18

food, 14, 16

habitat, 6

polyps, 18, 20

sizes, 8

tentacles, 14, 16

young, 20

Word Count: 159
Grade: 1
Early-Intervention Level: 12